Faith Begins at
DAD

In the space of just a few pages, this resource contains a wealth of helpful and insightful ways that dads can invest in their kids' spiritual wellbeing. No matter how busy you are, it's worth reading!

Jim Daly
President and CEO, Focus on the Family

As a senior pastor, Mark Holmen demonstrated how a local church can inspire and equip families to instill strong faith in the next generation. As a partner in the Strong Families Innovation Alliance, he has also been a mentor to other leaders trying to turn the tide of declining generational faith transference.

Kurt Bruner
Executive Director, Strong Families Innovation Alliance

Mark Holmen is energizing families to grow their faith in the home. Mark and his message is one of the freshest and most practical voices among Christian leaders. This resource is helping us follow the mandate of God to pass on our faith from generation to generation.

Jim Burns, Ph.D.
President, HomeWord
Senior Director of the Center for Youth and Family at Azusa Pacific University

Mark Holmen pulls no punches as he directly challenges the hearts of dads to lead in the home as God intended. *Faith Begins @ Home Dad* is for real men. If you dare to pick it up, be ready to be used by God to make a real difference in the faith formation of your kids.

Pastor Greg McCombs
Director of the Canadian Marriage & Family Network
Faith@Home Coach

Mark Holmen clearly knows what spiritual development in the family should look like, and he knows how to communicate that message in a warm, transparent and engaging way. Parents who digest the four Faith Begins @ Home booklets will have their vision lifted, their hearts warmed, and their minds focused on the practical things they can do to see their children embrace Christ for a lifetime. I recommend these resources to every believing family.

Richard Ross, Ph.D.
Professor of Student Ministry at Southwestern Seminary
Fort Worth, Texas

Mark Holmen is providing much-needed leadership in the Faith@Home movement that is sweeping our nation. These resources are excellent tools in that they both challenge and equip parents as they seek to disciple their own children.

Steve Stroope
Lead Pastor, Lake Pointe Church
Rockwall, Texas

Mark Holmen

Author, *Faith Begins at Home* and Founder of Faith @ Home Ministries

Faith Begins
@Home
DAD

Regal

From Gospel Light
Ventura, California, U.S.A.

Published by Regal
From Gospel Light
Ventura, California, U.S.A.
www.regalbooks.com
Printed in the U.S.A.

Library of Congress Cataloging-in-Publication Data
Holmen, Mark.
Faith begins @ home dad / Mark Holmen.
p. cm.
ISBN 978-0-8307-5230-0 (trade paper)
1. Families—Religious life. 2. Fatherhood—Religious aspects—
Christianity. 3. Parenting—Religious aspects—Christianity.
4. Child rearing—Religious aspects--Christianity. I. Title.
II. Title: Faith at home dad.
BV4526.3.H647 2010
248.8'421—dc22
2009044684

1 2 3 4 5 6 7 8 9 10 / 16 15 14 13 12 11 10

Rights for publishing this book outside the U.S.A. or in
non-English languages are administered by Gospel Light Worldwide, an international not-for-profit ministry.
For additional information, please visit www.glww.org,
email info@glww.org, or write to Gospel Light Worldwide,
1957 Eastman Avenue, Ventura, CA 93003, U.S.A.

I dedicate this resource to my dad, Arlen,
who went to be with the Lord in the fall of 2004.
Thanks, Dad, for being a focused faith-at-home
dad who showed me how to enjoy living life as
a Christian 24 hours a day, 7 days a week.
I miss you lots and love you even more.

Contents

Introduction

This book is for all fathers, everywhere. But if you're a brand-new dad or a soon-to-be dad, then congratulations! I have some great advice and encouragement that can make fatherhood a true joy from the very beginning and help you leave the kind of legacy you can be proud of.

I remember when I became a dad. We were in a birthing room of a hospital in Minnesota. I had come prepared. I had a boom box (this was before iPods) with lots of music, playing cards, a video camera, a regular camera, snacks, bottled water, diet Coke and many things intended to serve as my wife's focal point. I was ready! It was October 30, 1995. About 10:30 P.M., the pushing began. I was by my wife's side every minute. Unfortunately, at 11:50, I made the big mistake of saying, "Honey, push hard. We don't want to have a baby born on Halloween." My wife gave me "The Look," which said, "Shut up unless you want to get down here and do this yourself!"

In that moment, I learned an important lesson: Never give your wife advice while she's in the last stages of labor.

At 12:13 A.M., October 31, Malyn Mae Holmen was born. Yes, we had a Halloween baby, and we nicknamed her Boo Boo. We have loved having birthday parties on October 31, so my fears of having a Halloween baby were unfounded.

When Malyn was born, the nurses instantly took her to the other side of the room to check her over. There I was, standing between my wife and my newborn. On one side, my wife was moaning in pain. On the other side, my daughter was screaming. I didn't know which way to go. I had been a dad for only seconds and I already needed help. Thankfully, I heard the voice of the Lord, which sounded a lot like my wife's voice, say, "Go make sure Malyn is okay."

If you're a new father and feeling even a little overwhelmed or concerned about being a dad, I understand. I'm not going to make you admit publicly that you have no clue or that you are scared to death about parenting a baby who will become a child and then a teenager, and eventually a young adult who may never move out of your house. However, I am going to be very direct with you. When my dad had something serious to talk about, he would say, "Mark, let's talk man-to-man for a minute." In this booklet I intend to talk man-to-man with you. No holding punches. No wives around. I simply want to be ruthlessly honest about the most important thing you will do with your life in the days, weeks, months and years ahead.

Who am I to offer you any advice? No one. How's that for a selling point? In many ways I feel like Paul when he wrote in Ephesians 3:7-8:

"I became a servant of this gospel by the gift of God's grace given me through the working of his power. Although I am less than the least of all God's people, this grace was given me."

It is only by the grace of God that I am a husband, father, pastor and author. I am simply a dad just like you. I have had the opportunity to serve in four congregations over the last 20 years, working with thousands of parents and children. I've had the opportunity to see good dads and not-so-good dads. I've seen dads that have set the bar so high that I can only wish to be the type of dad they are. I have seen dads who have set the bar so low that I already looked like a world champion parent before my daughter was even born.

In this booklet are some key things to consider that will help you connect with your kids on a deeper spiritual level. You may not agree with everything I say, and that is okay. I simply want you to begin wrestling with some of these things so you won't look back at your life one day and say, "I wish someone would have told me."

Throughout each chapter you will find some "Let's Talk Man-to-Man" questions to challenge you or use as discussion questions with a group of men if you choose to go through this booklet with some other dads. The Bible, and especially Deuteronomy 6, will serve as the foundation for each chapter. Deuteronomy 6 speaks specifically to parents—to dads. You don't have to do everything perfectly as a dad. All I'm asking is for you to be open and willing to let God shape you into the great dad you can become.

1

The Benefits of Being a Focused Dad

These are the commands, decrees and laws the Lord your God directed me to teach you to observe in the land that you are crossing the Jordan to possess, so that you, your children and their children after them may fear the Lord your God as long as you live by keeping all his decrees and commands that I give you, and so that you may enjoy long life.

DEUTERONOMY 6:1-2

There is nothing worse for a man than to be embarrassed or made to look foolish simply because he doesn't have the right information. On the flip side, there is nothing better than knowing he has inside information about something he can use against his buddies.

I remember that in college we had a guy who lived on our dorm floor who was a huge moocher. He had an uncanny ability to show up to your dorm room the second you received your pizza delivery, taking as many pieces of pizza as you would allow. If you left a bag of chips or cookies out that your mom sent you, they were sure to be quickly in the hands and stomach of the dorm moocher. He never seemed to have food of his own, and all he did every evening was walk around from room to room looking for food he could mooch off of others.

After awhile, we had had enough. We decided to do something about it. Each of us booby-trapped our food by replacing the Oreo cookie filling with toothpaste, putting laxative in the brownie mix, grinding hot peppers onto the pizza and putting five-day-old cold coffee inside our liter Coke bottles. It was amazing and somewhat scary to see how creative we were at turning ordinary looking food into weapons of mass destruction! Throughout the weekend our mooching buddy, not knowing that we were all in this together, was greeted with surprise after surprise. For us it was fun, but for our buddy who wasn't "in the know" it became a very long weekend with many trips to the bathroom.

What does this story have to do with being a good dad? Would you rather be in the know or not in the know when it comes to being a good dad? I would rather have the inside information instead of walking through life saying, "Why didn't somebody tell me?"

Keep reading, and before you're finished, you will be in the know. It will change the course of your life.

The Choice Is Yours

In the first verse of Deuteronomy 6, Moses says, "These are the commands, decrees, and laws the LORD your God directed me to teach you." You already have the information you need to be a good dad. You cannot say it wasn't given to you. God has consistently and repeatedly told you, in His Word, what you need to know and do to be a good dad: Do not covet, do not commit adultery, do not steal, lie, cheat, defraud, and so on. Love God; love others. Forgive as you have been forgiven. Do not worship other gods. Don't swear, murder or discredit others. Do I need to go further? (For a refresher, read Exodus 20; Matthew 22:36-40; Luke 6:37.)

You simply need to do life God's way. You already know how to be a good dad. You really do. The knowledge is in you. In fact, you were created to be a good, faithful, obedient and godly dad. God has very clearly explained it.

The key word in Deuteronomy 6:1 is "observe." "Observe" is more than just watching. It means accepting and actively engaging and participating in. It's like when you get pulled over for speeding and you say to the police officer, "I didn't know what the speed limit was," which never works for guys, by the way. You knew the speed limit. You simply chose not to observe it. That is what most dads today do. It is not a lack of knowledge or understanding of what to do. The problem comes in knowingly choosing not to observe what you need to do. Unfortunately, as you know, if you continue to not observe the speed limit, it's just a matter of time until you pay the consequences. It's the same with being a dad who does not follow God's way, except that the consequences are eternal.

Let's Talk Man-to-Man

- Dad, are you going to be the man who observes life God's way, or are you going to ignore God's way?
- You have been given the greatest gift you could ever be given: a son or daughter. What are you going to do with this gift?
- What example will you set for your child?
- How are you going to live your life, and what will your children remember about you?

You have only two options: living your life God's way or living life your way. It's a choice every dad faces. What is your choice?

"So That" Benefits

A seminary professor once told our class to take notice and even circle whenever we saw a "so that" in the Bible, because what is coming next is a significant point. In Deuteronomy 6:2, two "so that" statements identify significant points that we must not miss.

The first point is, "So that you, your children and their children after them . . ." *The choice you make to live life God's way or not will not only impact you but will also impact your children and grandchildren.*

Dr. David Anderson asked a question in his opening remarks at a workshop on "How to Pass On Faith to Your Teenagers": "How many of you wish your teenager had a stronger faith?" Every hand in the room went up. Then he dropped the bomb. "Realize, that what you are seeing in your teenager's faith is, in all likelihood, a mirror image of your faith." I expected everyone to be angry and ready to leave, but instead, people were nodding in agreement.

I've had many dads in my office over the years say they wished they could have a "do over" with their children. "If I could do it over again I would have taken my Christian walk more seriously when I was raising my children. I had no idea how much impact the way I lived my life, and the choices I was making, had on my kids."

Dad, if you choose to lie, cheat, deceive, steal, murder, swear and live according to the world's "get what you can while you can" rules, it will have multigenerational impact on your children and beyond. If you choose to live according to the Lord's ways, where you love unconditionally, forgive graciously, honor respectfully, serve generously and sacrifice willingly, you will have multigenerational impact that will bear fruit for generations to come.

Let's Talk Man-to-Man

- What do you think when you hear that your child's faith will be a mirror image of your faith?
- Have you ever wished you could have a "do over"? What's one thing you would do over if you could?
- What type of faith would you like your children and grandchildren to have?

The second "so that" statement in Deuteronomy 6:2 is, "So that you may enjoy long life." *God wants you, your children and your grandchildren to enjoy long life.*

Many men have the wrong impression of God. They think God is a big judge sitting in heaven waiting to zap people when they do something wrong. That is not the God of the Bible. God desperately wants you, your children and your children's children to enjoy long life. And realize when Moses wrote about the "so that" consequences, he was not just talking about 80 or 90 years here on earth. Moses was talking about eternal life. God wants you and your children and grandchildren to spend eternity with Him in heaven.

God's ways are designed to lead you and your children and your children's children into eternal life. Do you want to live eternally in a place where there is no pain, suffering, tears, mourning or death? Do you want to live eternally free from the sinful conditions of this world that have held us captive? Do you want this for your children and your grandchildren? The decision you make to live life God's way or not has not only multigenerational impact, but it also has eternal consequences. It's a big deal!

Dad, I told you that I wasn't going to hold any punches. The decision you are now facing to be a God-following dad has eternal consequences for you, your precious child and your future grandchildren. How you choose to live your life will be the primary thing that opens or closes the door for your child to spend eternity in heaven.

I know there are a lot of things you want for your children right now. You may want them to be a basketball player, a golfer and a lover of pepperoni pizza, like you. You may have already bought them their first Cubs uniform, basketball hoop or racecar set. You may already have them signed up for Tae Kwon Do or hockey and have plans to watch them win the Olympics. While these are all well-intentioned dreams, are they really the most important things you want to pass on to your children? Is having a hunting partner or fellow Bears fan really what is most important to you?

The Bottom Line

Jesus was clear about those who wanted to follow Him setting their priorities. He said that anyone who wanted to follow Him would be willing to let go of worldly things and follow Him. Then He asked, "What good will it be for a man if he gains the whole world, yet forfeits his soul?" (Matthew 16:26). What good would it be if your children shared all your worldly interests with you but lost out on eternity with God because you didn't share spiritual things with them too?

How about this question: Do you want your children to end up in heaven or hell? That's a serious and real question. Whether you want to admit it or not, death is inevitable and there is an eternal destination after death where we will all end up. Matthew 25:31-46 paints a very clear picture of what is going to happen in the future.

> When the Son of Man comes in his glory, and all the angels with him, he will sit on his throne in heavenly glory. All the nations will be gathered before him, and he will separate the people one from another as a shepherd separates the sheep from the goats. He will put the sheep on his right and the goats on his left.
>
> Then the King will say to those on his right, "Come, you who are blessed by my Father; take your inheritance, the kingdom prepared for you since the creation of the world. For I was hungry and you gave me something to eat, I was thirsty and you gave me something to drink, I was a stranger and you invited me in, I needed clothes and you clothed me, I was sick and you looked after me, I was in prison and you came to visit me."

Then the righteous will answer him, "Lord, when did we see you hungry and feed you, or thirsty and give you something to drink? When did we see you a stranger and invite you in, or needing clothes and clothe you? When did we see you sick or in prison and go to visit you?"

The King will reply, "I tell you the truth, whatever you did for one of the least of these brothers of mine, you did for me."

Then he will say to those on his left, "Depart from me, you who are cursed, into the eternal fire prepared for the devil and his angels. For I was hungry and you gave me nothing to eat, I was thirsty and you gave me nothing to drink, I was a stranger and you did not invite me in, I needed clothes and you did not clothe me, I was sick and in prison and you did not look after me."

They also will answer, "Lord, when did we see you hungry or thirsty or a stranger or needing clothes or sick or in prison, and did not help you?"

He will reply, "I tell you the truth, whatever you did not do for one of the least of these, you did not do for me."

Then they will go away to eternal punishment, but the righteous to eternal life.

There will be a dividing time when God sets apart those who chose to follow His ways. Here's the deal, dad: You can raise your children to be a Cubs fan, a soccer star, an avid hunter, a straight *A* student or a successful business leader, but if they end up spending eternity in hell, will you be proud of what you did?

When Christ returns, which is going to happen, do you want to see your children sent into eternal punishment, or would you like to see them brought into eternal life? This is heavy, but it is reality. You have a child now, and the type of life you choose to observe will have multigenerational, eternal ramifications.

The apostle Paul never stopped straining forward for what was ahead, pressing on "toward the goal to win the prize" for which God had called him "heavenward in Christ Jesus" (Philippians 3:14). As a dad, never stop straining forward in this life. Remember that as you move forward, you take with you those precious children God gave you to show them the path they can take too. As they strain forward, they will be leading your grandchildren in the same path. What a legacy!

Let's Talk Man-to-Man

- What is the most important thing you want to pass on to your child(ren)?
- How would you feel if your child were to end up in hell? Is your child's eternal destiny something you have even considered?
- What are you willing to do so that you, your children and grandchildren will one day enter eternal life in heaven?

2

Listen Up!

Hear, O Israel, and be careful to obey so that it may go well with you and that you may increase greatly in a land flowing with milk and honey, just as the LORD, the God of your fathers, promised you. Hear, O Israel: The LORD our God, the LORD is one. Love the LORD your God with all your heart and with all your soul and with all your strength. These commandments that I give you today are to be upon your hearts.

DEUTERONOMY 6:3-6

Be Careful to Obey God

Deuteronomy 6:3-6 has two instructions you need to be the great dad God created you to be. The first, "be careful to obey so that it may go well with you," is a "so that" statement. Have you thought about what God wants? God wants things to go well for you. Don't ever lose sight of that. God's way is not boring, confining or arduous; it's what leads to you enjoying long life. Do you want to enjoy long life, a life that is so much longer than 80 to 90 years on earth? Do you want a life that will give you all of eternity to explore the vastness of God's creation, of which we can only see a minute portion now? That doesn't sound boring to me.

What is the condition that makes it possible for things to go well for you as a dad so that you may enjoy long life? *Be careful to obey*.

It is so tempting to not obey. From an early age you were tempted to not obey your parents, teachers, leaders and, later, your bosses. While you might say, "If I were Eve I would have never eaten that forbidden fruit," the truth of the matter is that you eat that same forbidden fruit almost every day! Have you obeyed God today with every thought, word and deed? Me neither. I know exactly where Paul is coming from when he writes in Romans 7:15, "I do not understand what I do. For what I want to do I do not do, but what I hate I do." You want to obey, but it's just plain difficult. And that's because the easy road is the road called disobedience. It's so much easier to disobey than it is to obey. And there is also something that seems courageous and exhilarating about disobeying. Yet the fact of the matter is simply this: If you disobey God's way, there are consequences to pay. Just ask Eve!

It's time to man up and start doing life God's way, which by the way isn't a bad thing since it leads to your enjoying long eternal life! But you're a dad now and another life is going to be influenced by you. So quit whining, lying, cheating, stealing, lusting, gambling, ranting, raving, misbehaving, swearing, coveting, dishonoring, disrespecting and any other thing that is not of God, and start living according to WWJHYD so that it may go well with you. What is WWJHYD?

Remember those bracelets and T-shirts with the letters WWJD printed on them? WWJD stands for What Would Jesus Do? I have added two letters so it reads WWJHYD—What Would Jesus Have You Do? Imagine if we all lived by that question! When someone cuts you off on the interstate and flips you the bird, what would Jesus have you do? When you are away from home on a business trip and the opportunity to watch pornographic movies presents itself, what would Jesus have you do? When your buddies invite you to spend a weekend in Las Vegas living according to the motto, "What happens in Vegas stays in Vegas," what would Jesus have you do? When you have a chance to cheat on your taxes, what would Jesus have you do? When your wife asks you on Saturday night if you're going to go to church on Sunday, what would Jesus have you do?

Let's play this out to see if doing life God's way is confining, boring or arduous. If you disobey and don't do life God's way, you end up being a road-raging, porn-addicted adulterer with a tax evasion lawsuit, and you don't go to church. Boy, doesn't that sound fun! Is that the type of dad you want to be?

Now let's play it out according to God's way. When you are careful to obey, you are living according to WWJHYD. You end up being a peace-filled, promise-keeping, oath-honoring, trustworthy, honest, wise, church-going man. It goes well with you. How does that sound to you?

Let's Talk Man-to-Man

- What words come to mind when you think of God? What are some characteristics of God?
- What words best describe you? What are some of your characteristics?
- How would living according to WWJHYD impact and/or change how you currently live your life?
- How do those changes sound to you?

The Deuteronomy 6 passage intensifies as Moses twice says, "Hear, O Israel!" Imagine him saying this in the same manner as a pulpit-pounding preacher would and replace "O Israel" with your name. It would sound something like, "Listen up, Jim . . . Mike . . . John . . . Jordan . . . Antonio . . . José! Now that I have your attention, there is something of huge importance that you need to know and embrace." "The LORD our God, the LORD is one. Love the LORD your God with all your heart and with all your soul and with all your strength. These commandments that I give you today are to be upon your hearts" (vv. 4-6).

There is only one true God. There aren't multiple gods or choices for you to worship or follow. There is only one—the Three in One: Father, Son and Holy

Spirit. Don't fall for what anyone else is selling you regarding other gods or paths to heaven. There is only one. It may not be politically correct to say, but it is the truth, plain and simple. It is through God—Father, Son and Holy Spirit—that you, your children and your children's children will come to enjoy long, everlasting life. Disobey this truth and you pay.

Love God with Everything in You

Love the Lord your God with all your heart and with all your soul and with all your strength. Are you ready for a tough series of questions?

- Do you love God?
- Are you in love with God?
- Do you live in a manner that shows that you are in love with God?
- Would your wife, friends, coworkers and, in the future, children say that you are in love with God?

One speaker I heard challenged us to go home and ask our kids to tell us who they thought we were in love with. The point was to see whether God made the list. A few days later, after picking up my daughter from school, I asked her, "Malyn, who do I love?" She was caught by surprise, so I asked it again. "This isn't a trick question, I just would like to know who you think I love." I must confess that for a moment I wish I would have never taken this challenge, because my daughter was a very honest 13-year-old! But in a defining moment for me, my daughter responded without hesitating, "That's easy, Daddy. You love God, Mommy and me." I let out a huge sigh of relief, and yet that question continues to drive me today. Your children will know who you love based on how you live.

In this Deuteronomy passage, Moses is clearly saying, "Dad, you need to live in a loving relationship with God." In other words, it is not just enough to know about God; you need to be in love with God. You need to love Him with *all* of your heart, soul and strength. You may be wondering how that's possible. It is possible because God became Someone in Jesus Christ, that we could fall in love with. God showed how a Father loves a Son and how He loves us: "God so loved the world that he gave his one and only Son, that whoever believes in him shall not perish but have eternal life. For God did not send his Son into the world to condemn the world, but to save the world through him" (John 3:16-17). We love Him because He first loved us (see 1 John 4:19).

I want you to think for a minute about the guys you love. I know I'm treading on thin ice here because some guys have difficulty admitting or saying they love another guy, but you need to get over that. I love Tim, Andrew, Doug, Brian, Warren, Matt, Mark, Dave and Bob, and I don't have a problem admitting it. I love them because we have gone through life together and have been there for each other. I like spending time with these guys because I know them and feel comfortable around them. I must ask myself the difficult questions, "Do I love Jesus as much as I love these guys? Do I know Jesus as much as I know these guys? Do I spend as much time with Jesus as I do with these guys?"

Your child is going to love who you love. If you are not in love with Jesus, and you are not living in a manner that reflects you are in love with Jesus—meaning you are spending time with Him—your child in all likelihood will not be in love with Jesus. And remember, it's a loving relationship with Jesus Christ that leads you, your children and your grandchildren into enjoying long, eternal life.

A friend of mine is a children's pastor in Portland, Oregon, and he has two grown daughters who are both strong Christians today. Recently he was intrigued to find out why his daughters remained strong Christians instead of turning away from Christianity as many young adults do. He went to both of them separately and asked them a simply question; "Could you tell me why you are a Christian today? What were some things that helped you become the Christian you are today?" His daughters were two years apart and they were very different from one another, yet he was stunned when both of them gave the very same answer. He said, "This may have been the first time they ever agreed on something, and maybe that's because they didn't even know they were saying the same thing, because I asked them separately." What was the reason? "Dad, I can tell you why I'm a Christian. Every day when I would come to breakfast I always knew that you would be there at the kitchen table reading the Bible. You never wavered from your faith and commitment to God, and that's why I never have or will either."

There you have it, Dad. If you want your children to enjoy eternal life, it's about you and your faith. If you want your kids to have a strong prayer life, then strengthen your prayer life. If you want your kids to make godly decisions, then you need to make godly decisions. If you want your kids to love unconditionally, then you need to love unconditionally. If you want them to serve and obey God, then you need to serve and obey God. You can't pass something on to your kids that you don't have yourself.

Let's Talk Man-to-Man

- So, what are you thinking right now? Especially when you hear that you can't pass something on to your kids that you don't have yourself?
- On a scale of 1 to 10, how close would you say you are to God (1 being not close at all; 10 being extremely close)?
- What are some things you could begin doing that would help you know and love God better?

3

"Impress Them"

Impress them [commandments] on your children. Talk about them when you sit at home and when you walk along the road, when you lie down and when you get up. Tie them as symbols on your hands and bind them on your foreheads. Write them on the doorframes of your houses and on your gates.

DEUTERONOMY 6:7-9

Firsthand Impressions

The word "impress" in this Deuteronomy passage literally means to be permanently branded or established. The ways of God are to be permanently branded or established on the hearts and minds of your children. They are not something your kids memorize, recite and forget. The ways and commands of God are to be permanently fixed so that your children live according to them naturally, without even having to think about it.

What impresses you? I'm impressed by a lot of things. I was impressed when I had a chance to watch Tiger Woods practice on a driving range before a golf tournament. I was impressed with how easily he could hit the ball farther and more consistently than I could imagine.

I was impressed and completely in awe of God when I saw the Grand Canyon for the first time. And I was truly impressed the first time I walked into Wrigley Field to see the Chicago Cubs play. I still remember exactly where I sat and how green the grass was and how beautiful the ivy was in center field. I have seen Tiger Woods, the Grand Canyon and Wrigley Field many times on television, but it wasn't the same. What makes a lasting impression? Seeing something firsthand with your own eyes.

You can tell your children the ways and commands of God. You can take your children to church and have the church teach them the ways and commands of God. But your children will not have a lasting impression of the commands of God until they see them firsthand in you.

Dad, whether you like to hear this or not, your children is going to be impressed, one way or the other, by the way you live your life. You can impress them to be one-hour-a-week-at church-only (hypocritical) Christians, who only dress, act, and behave like Christians at church, or you can impress them to be fully devoted, 24/7 Christians who are continually living according to the question WWJHYD?— What Would Jesus Have You Do?

Authentic Faith

"Dear friends, remember what the apostles of our Lord Jesus Christ foretold. They said to you, 'In the last times there will be scoffers who will follow their own ungodly desires.' These are the men who divide you, who follow mere natural instincts and do not have the Spirit. But you, dear friends, build yourselves up in your most holy faith and pray in the Holy Spirit. Keep yourselves in God's love as you wait for the mercy of our Lord Jesus Christ to bring you to eternal life" (Jude 1:17-21).

Men do not want to be called hypocrites. They do not want their children to be hypocrites. Yet hypocrisy is the number-one reason why many young adults, who were Christians as teenagers, walk away from the faith. A variety of research indicates that anywhere between 60 percent to 90 percent of current Christian teenagers are going to walk away from the faith when they are young adults.

Why? The primary reason cited is hypocrisy. They were dragged to church on Sunday morning where they were made to act, live and behave one way at church; but at home they lived a completely different lifestyle where the name of Jesus was never mentioned and there was no prayer, Bible reading or family devotions. These children were raised to believe that Christianity is something you do at church, not at home or any other time. When they became young adults they walked away, saying, "If this is what Christianity is then I don't want anything to do with it."

I was dragged to church on Sunday mornings, many times against my will. I was made to go to Sunday School and confirmation class and youth group. I couldn't wait until I was old enough to choose for myself; and at that time, I walked away from church. What kept me in my Christian faith, even when I wandered for a period of time, was the example that my mom and dad continually set for me at home. My mom and dad lived out their faith 24/7 at home. They weren't perfect, but they were authentic. They lived for God, followed God, prayed to God, wrestled through difficulties with God and did life God's way to the very best of their ability. Even as I wandered, they stayed the course. I never saw hypocritical Christian living out of them. I saw hypocrites at church, lots of them, to be honest. But I never experienced hypocritical living at home; and that, I believe, is the primary reason why I am still following God today.

Let's Talk Man-to-Man

- Do you know any hypocritical Christians? If so, how did they impact your view and understanding of God?
- What was your attitude toward church when you were growing up?
- Who are people you would consider to be authentic Christians? What is it about them or their lifestyle that leaves this impression on you?
- Are you living the type of life that will leave the impression that you are an authentic Christian?

I know you don't want your children to blame your hypocritical lifestyle for the reason they abandon faith in God. You can choose today to be the type of dad who will impress your children to be authentic followers of Christ. This passage from Deuteronomy outlines three things you can do to impress your children with authentic faith—talk about God, display everyday faith and invite Jesus into your home.

Talk Often About God

"Talk about them when you sit at home and when you walk along the road, when you lie down and when you get up" (Deuteronomy 6:7).

First, simply talk about God and His ways at home. The only time many men talk about God is at church. That simply will not do. You must follow the instruction of Moses and talk about faith with your children in the home. It has to be a part of your everyday vocabulary.

Unfortunately, statistics show that when it comes to impressing faith on children through faith-talk we have some serious work to do. Search Institute conducted a nationwide survey of over 11,000 participants from 561 congregations across 6 different denominations.[1] The results are revealing.

- The percentage of youth who have a regular dialogue with their mother on faith/life issues: 12 percent

- The percentage of youth who have a regular dialogue with their father on faith/life issues: 5 percent
- The percentage of youth who have experienced regular reading of the Bible and devotions in the home: 9 percent
- The percentage of youth who have experienced a servanthood event with a parent as an action of faith: 12 percent

George Barna further confirmed this reality in his book *Transforming Children into Spiritual Champions*. He wrote, "We discovered that in a typical week, fewer than 10 percent of parents who regularly attend church with their kids read the Bible together, pray together (other than at meal times) or participate in an act of service as a family unit. Even fewer families—1 out of ever 20—have any type of worship experience together with their kids, other than while they are at church during a typical month."[2]

Dads need to be talking about and living out true faith with their children. If you remember nothing else from this book, please remember this: *Faith is not something that can be taught, faith is something that must be caught.* It's like catching a cold. When my daughter catches a cold at school and brings it into our home, my wife, Maria, and I both catch the cold. That's how it is with faith. If faith-talk is in the home, everyone catches it. Get faith talk into your everyday life and not just on Sunday mornings.

When Moses says to talk about these things when you lie down and when you get up, he means all the time. Everything you go through on a day-to-day basis is an opportunity to talk about faith and walk with God. The key to faith-talk, as Moses describes, is not having all the answers; the key is having the conversations. In these conversations you "train a child in the way he should go, and when he is old he will not turn from it" (Proverbs 22:6).

Think about all the times throughout the day and the week that you are with your children. Some days you may spend more time with them than other days because of your schedule, their schedule and other responsibilities. Write down what each day looks like, including the hours you are at work and at home. For the times when you are at home, list all the other things you need to take care of. Are any of these times when you could include your kids? Even very young children could help you wash the car, sort laundry or hand you tools as you worked on projects. It may take a little longer with them around, but view these as opportunities to build your relationship with your children and engage them in conversation. Don't expect big discussions each time. Have a listening ear for what they are interested in talking about. Lead the conversation to things of God as you integrate your faith with the topics of life.

Include times in your schedule when you are available to your children, not always off doing something else. From the time your children are very young, be with your children every day, if just for a few minutes. Play with them, read to them, cuddle them, change their diapers, feed them, get into their world. As their dad, you will be the first image they get about their loving heavenly Father.

As your children grow older, change your play with their changing interests. If you wait to develop a relationship until your children are teenagers and expect to have spiritual conversations with them, you may find that door already closed. They've been watching and learning all through the years.

In your schedule, when you block out time for Bible reading and prayer, do it some of the time when the kids are still awake where they can see you spending time with God. Occasionally share with them what you're reading in the Bible and what you're discovering about God. Sometimes include them in your prayer time so they can see what your relationship with God is like. You may want to shorten it from what you would regularly do, but your model will help them know how to have a prayer time with God.

In my book *Faith Begins at Home*, I shared seven regular opportunities to engage in faith-talk with practical examples.

1. Car Time

Some people say that time with family in the car is the most they spend together. Take advantage of these minutes to build faith in your children.

- Try turning off the radio and talking to your children about areas they may be struggling with. Then take a moment to pray about it as you are headed to your next destination.

- Share stories with your children about times God has helped you with something.

- Ask your children what questions they have for God. Spend a few moments talking about what God's answers might be, based on what He has revealed in the Bible about Himself.

- Speculate together about what heaven might be like.

- Look out the car window and try to find as many different kinds of God's creation as possible.

- Sing songs of praise, and worship together as you travel. Ask your kids what their favorite songs are and sing those together.

- Listen to audiotapes or CDs. You can probably check out from your local library recorded Christian stories or Bible stories.

- With older children, talk about movies that you've seen together and discuss lifestyles and decisions the characters made.

Speculate how the movie might have been different if the people had made different decisions. Compare ideas and philosophies of the movie with that of the Bible. These discussions with older children and teenagers will help them to think about and evaluate what they see and hear.

2. Bedtime

There is no better time to talk about faith than at bedtime. Your presence and love helps shape your children's first concepts of God.

- Make bedtime a regular time to spend with your kids. Be aware of the time and make an effort to stop what you're doing to be with them.

- With young children, read from a Bible storybook and sing songs together that teach them about God's love. They are never too young to begin to hear you talk about Jesus.

- With older children, share your highs and lows from the day and then take time to pray for each other.

- With teenagers ask, "What's on your schedule tomorrow that I can pray for? Do any of your friends need prayer for anything?" Talk through the hypocritical things they are seeing in the lives of teens who attend church and their school. Pray for these young people and talk about ways to be consistent with your faith at home, school and church. Discuss the difference between being a hypocrite and being an imperfect human. Encourage your teens to continue to go to God for forgiveness when they fail and not get down on themselves about it.

· Occasionally just sit with your children and wait. Often they will have something on their mind they will eventually begin to talk about. Listen and ask questions to get them to talk about it more. For older children, ask if they are interested in hearing your thoughts about it.

· Select good books and spend a part of your bedtime routine reading a chapter or two. No child is too old to be read to. When your children can read, have them take turns reading to you. Talk for a few minutes about what you read.

· Spend time together each evening list five things from the day that each of you are thankful to God for.

3. Meal Time

My parents would always pray before every meal, no matter where we were eating. Taking a moment to give God thanks and praise before eating establishes a ritual that remains with children into adulthood.

- Use mealtimes to listen to how everyone's day went. Before you leave the table, you may want to sometimes end your time together praying for one another.

- Tell funny stories. Laughter bonds people together. During your day, think about funny things you can share at mealtime. When your children feel connected to you, they will be more open to share with you and receive your words.

- Use sentence starters to get your children talking about faith, e.g., "If I lived when Jesus lived, I would . . ." "When I get to heaven, I would like to . . ." "If I could invite someone from the Bible to eat a meal with our family, it would be . . . because . . ." "My favorite part of God's creation is . . ."

- As your children grow older, tell them what strengths and abilities you see in them and the skills you see them developing. Talk about what kinds of ways God might want to use these. Pray with them for God's guidance for their future.

- Tell stories about your childhood. Tell your children what you're thankful for from your growing-up years and what you wish had been different. Ask your children to share things they are thankful for and what changes they would like to see. Pray together about these things. If changes can be made, consider what you might do.

- Tell your children how you see them growing in all ways. Let them know you are proud of the good choices they make and you are confident they are growing into young men and women of God.

- Talk to your young children about where the food you are eating comes from. Start all the way back to the food's origin, e.g., from the seed in the dirt. Make connections to God's provision of food even though all they may know is that it comes from the refrigerator or the store. After you've explained it a few times, ask them to tell you where a food you are eating comes from.

4. Vacation Time

Vacation time is a perfect time to reestablish faith-talk in your family. Tithe 10 percent of your vacation time to God.

· Do a family service project. Maybe even choose a vacation spot sometime based on an opportunity to serve together.

· Take some quiet time to read the Bible or have a family devotion each day.

· Visit another church and discuss what you liked and disliked. How did this church compare to your church?

· If you travel, talk about the variety in God's creation in different places you visit.

· Take pictures and make a photo album of your trip with each family member contributing a memory and a Scripture verse that was meaningful on the trip. Let younger ones dictate to you and write it down for them.

· Talk about the differences of travel in Bible times, e.g., when God told Abram to move and the whole family picked up their belongings and animals and walked for many days to a whole new region. Ask questions that put the story into your lives: What kinds of things might God ask of you, and would you be willing to pick up everything and move? How do you know when you're hearing God's voice to do something? Share with your children how God has guided you in the past.

- On vacation, you will have lots of opportunities to be an example of how to treat others. Be kind and generous to waiters and waitresses. Be a considerate—and patient—driver. Vacations can be the best of times—and the worst of times. Your character will come through loud and clear through it all. When you mess up, don't be afraid to admit it, and when necessary, ask your kids to forgive you. After all, you want them to be humble and work out problems, too, right?

- On the last evening of your vacation have a time of prayer/worship where you listen to a couple of contemporary Christian songs, and then take some time to give thanks for the time you had together. Share with each other one thing you were thankful for and one thing you look forward to when you get home.

5. Sick Time

Some of the most significant blocks of time that you have with your children are when they are home sick. While sick time isn't something that we look forward to—and there will certainly be some times when talking won't be the best idea—many times being under the weather will provide a time for healthy conversation.

- Watch videos together. Choose videos that could lead to dialogue about issues of faith and life.

- Read stories from the Bible about how Jesus treated sick people.

- Talk about the hope we have in heaven where there will be no suffering, pain or sickness.

- Pray for your sick child and believe God to heal, whether instantly, through medicine, or the healing process God designed in the body. Thank God for His care.

- Read a book together.

- Just sit and be together.

- Listen to music.

6. Memory Making Time

As a youth and family pastor, I had the opportunity to lead many youth service trips. These trips were usually a very positive and many times life changing experience for the teens as they experienced what it was like to be the hands and feet of Jesus and help people in their time of need. While I loved leading these service trips, I continued to wonder what could happen if the family shared this experience together. Occasionally my wife, daughter and I go down to the local homeless shelter and help sort food and serve the homeless. Each time this experience makes us more thankful for the many things we have been given that we could easily take for granted. When a family is having relational conflict my recommendation to them is to go out and do a service project together. Many times the experience of helping those less fortunate tends to put the problems your family is facing in a new perspective. I think it could be said that the family that serves together stays together.

- Help out a neighbor with lawn work. Even young children can pick up trash or leaves or help plant flowers.

- Make a meal together and take it to someone you know who is not able to make meals because of sickness or they have just come home with a brand-new baby. Let everyone in the family help with the preparations and go together to deliver the meal.

- Volunteer as a family to do cleanup or plant flowers or do whatever needs to be done around your church.

- Encourage a thankful heart in your children by writing notes to people who connect with your family in some significant way: teachers, neighbors, church staff and volunteers, daycare providers, friends, extended family members. Let each family

member contribute to the notes with words
or drawings and sign their name. Deliver
these personally, if possible, as a family.

- Check on the possibilities of serving at a
local mission, distributing food on a holi-
day or even on a regular day.

- Go to the pastor of your church and ask if
there is an individual or family they know
who could use some help. Maybe you could
adopt a senior citizen from your church
and help with things he or she needs done
around the house.

7. One-on-One Time

Maybe the best thing you can do is establish a ritual
of one-on-one time with each child. It may be
weekly or monthly, but build it into your life
rhythm. We have a refrigerator magnet that reads
"Don't should on yourself!" which reminds me to
do things now so that later I won't have to say, "I
should have done that." Every parent I know says
the same thing about parenting: "They grow up so
fast." It won't be long and you will be wondering
where the time went. A failure to make one-on-one
time now will leave you later in life saying, "I should
have done that." Every Friday until my daughter
reached school age was Daddy's Day. It was a day
my daughter knew I was all hers. We had a ritual of
going to McDonald's together, and we both looked

forward to it. Now that she is older, we have "Daddy time" which may be a weekend together or a date night where we go see a movie or have dinner together. The key is not the activity but the commitment to spend time together.

- Use part of your time together to talk about faith. Share what God has been teaching you as you read the Bible and talk with Him.

- Ask your children what kinds of things they have been learning spiritually.

- Share about areas in your life you would like to grow in.

- Decide to learn a few Bible verses together and use some of this time to practice saying a verse and talking about what it means to you.

- Enjoy each other's company and laugh together.

- Admire God's creation together at different times of the day and year.

- Tell your kids that sometimes things in the Bible or in life don't seem to make sense. Ask them what doesn't make sense to them. Be willing to explore these areas with your kids. You don't have to have all the answers. Part of your role is to help your kids know it's okay to ask questions and be honest about your thoughts.

• Take turns with your kids going back and forth completing this statement: "One of my favorite things is . . ." This not only let's you get to know each other better, but it also allows you to share your priorities with your kids in words. Doing this occasionally will become a routine they will enjoy, and you'll find that their favorite things will change over time. Knowing their interests will help you find ways to talk about spiritual things in their world.

• Dream together about what you would do if you had a whole week with nothing to do. Be open to discoveries through your children's expression. They might be the first ones to recognize and let you know that life is too hectic and there's not enough of your time left for them. Their needs will change as they grow older. Sometimes in life they will want to be with you more, sometimes less. Be available for all of their growing up. You'll never be back this way again. No do-overs.

Display Everyday Faith

"Tie them as symbols on your hands and bind them on your foreheads" (Deuteronomy 6:8). Wear your faith wherever you go. You have been called to be a godly man, not just at church and at home but everywhere you go. You are called to be a godly man at work by working as if you are working for the Lord. You are called to be a godly driver on the interstate when someone cuts you off. You are called to be a godly man in your basketball or hockey league as well as whenever no one is looking. Remember WWJHYD! What would Jesus have you do? Christianity is not something you simply turn on and off. You are called to be like Christ in all you do.

Occasionally ask your children and others who know you well how you are doing with consistency in your faith. "Do you see me acting at home like I do at church?" "Do I treat other drivers with patience and respect?" "At your sports and other events, do you see me living out my faith in Christ?"

Invite Jesus into Your Home

"Write them on the doorframes of your houses and on your gates" (Deuteronomy 6:9). Your home is a sanctuary where Christ resides. Do you view your home as a church? Have you heard parents scold their children at church by saying, "We don't do that at church"? This always makes me wonder, *So that behavior is okay at home?* Why is it okay to act one way at home and another at church?

The great painter Holman Hunt once painted a picture of Jesus knocking at a front door that was overgrown with vines. When he unveiled the picture a person commented that the picture was incomplete because Hunt had forgotten to put a doorknob on the door. Hunt responded, "I didn't forget. The handle is on the inside."

Dad, here's the deal. Jesus has been standing at the door of your home knocking, asking to come in. Jesus wants to reside with you. He doesn't want to be at church only. He wants to come into the center of your household to help positively impact your life 24 hours, 7 days a week. For some reason, it can be scary to think of Jesus being in your home. If you are doing some things in your house that you don't think Jesus would approve of, are those the type of things you want your children seeing? Imagine Jesus sitting on your couch. Would He impact what you watch on television? Imagine Jesus at your dining room table. Would He impact the discussions you have there? One family I know of sets an extra place at the kitchen table for every meal. It is the "Jesus place," and it serves to remind them that Jesus is there with them.

Jesus is with you always. He will help you as you live your faith at home. He will help you make faith-talk a part of your normal, everyday conversation. Wear your Christian faith wherever you go and bring Christ and Christ-like living into the center of your home. You will leave a lasting impression on your children that will change the course of their lives.

Let's Talk Man-to-Man

- What's harder/easier for you: talking about your faith or living out your faith?
- Who talked to you about faith when you were a child? What worked? What didn't work?
- Is Jesus living in your home? What would change about the way you live life at home if Jesus were in your home?

Notes

1. Reprinted with permission from *Effective Christian Education: A National Study of Protestant Congregations.* Copyright © 1990 by Search Institute SM. No other use is permitted without prior permission from Search Institute, 615 First Avenue NE, Minneapolis, MN 55413; www.search-institute.org.
2. George Barna, *Transforming Children into Spiritual Champions* (Ventura, CA: Regal Books, 2003), p. 78.

4

Be Careful

When the LORD your God brings you into the land he swore to your fathers, to Abraham, Isaac and Jacob, to give you—a land with large, flourishing cities you did not build, houses filled with all kinds of good things you did not provide, wells you did not dig, and vineyards and olive groves you did not plant—then when you eat and are satisfied, be careful that you do not forget the LORD, who brought you out of Egypt, out of the land of slavery. Fear the LORD your God, serve him only and take your oaths in his name. Do not follow other gods, the gods of the peoples around you.

DEUTERONOMY 6:10-14

Does anything in this passage sound familiar to you? Do you live in a city you didn't build? Do you have stuff in your house you have no idea where it came from? Do you drink water from a well you didn't dig? Do you have shrubs or trees in your yard you didn't plant? Do you have plenty to eat when you need it?

What's your point, Moses? "Be careful that you do not forget the LORD." Moses is clearly warning us to "not forget the Lord" and to "not follow other gods." God knows that when you live in a land of plenty, it is easy to follow other gods and forget the one true God and His ways. Have you ever forgotten God, especially when everything about your life is going really well? Have you ever followed other gods? Have you ever gotten out of balance by giving top priority to your own comforts? By thinking only about getting more money and more stuff? By neglecting your family and giving all your time away from work to a hobby or a sport?

Dangers in the Land of Plenty

I wish I could tell you that being a Christian dad is easy, but I can't. In fact, you probably already know it will be anything but easy. You are going to be continually tempted to turn from following God's ways. The primary source of temptation will come from the world. One of the dangers of living in the land of plenty is getting caught up in trying to live a plentiful life. Even though you have plenty, you want more. And the world keeps tempting you to have more, buy more, consume more, do more, become more. Because there is always more out there, you keep chasing after more things to do, have, achieve or become. You give and you strive.

This trap looks a lot like a treadmill. Once you get on, the treadmill keeps you going faster and faster until you have nothing left to give. Then the treadmill throws you off and says, "Who's next?" The world doesn't care about you. Do the gods that

are saying "If you just had a nicer car" really care
about you? What about the gods who say you need
to have a better-paying job or nicer house? Do they
really care about you or your children's eternity?
And what about the "What happens in Vegas stays
in Vegas" gods? Do they really care about the ramifications to you, your wife and your children? Why,
then, are the things of this world such a priority, especially when you know that the world doesn't give
a rip about you?

On the other hand, you have the one true God
of the universe who loves you and has plans to prosper you as a husband and father. And God's plans
for you are that you, your children and your children's children will enjoy long, everlasting, life . . .
remember?

> "I gave you a land on which you did not toil
> and cities you did not build; and you live in
> them and eat from vineyards and olive
> groves that you did not plant. Now fear the
> LORD and serve him with all faithfulness.
> Throw away the gods your forefathers wor-
> shiped beyond the River and in Egypt, and
> serve the LORD. But if serving the LORD
> seems undesirable to you, then choose for
> yourselves this day whom you will serve,
> whether the gods your forefathers served
> beyond the River, or the gods of the Amor-
> ites, in whose land you are living. But as for

me and my household, we will serve the
LORD." Then the people answered, "Far be
it from us to forsake the LORD to serve
other gods!" (Joshua 24:13-16).

I love this passage because it clearly shows us
the three things we need to do so that we won't forget the Lord.

Remember

Continually remember that everything you have is a
gift from God. You don't own anything. God is the
Provider and Source of it all. God gave you the food,
clothes, home and everything else you have. It is so
easy to forget this. It is easier to focus on everything
you don't have instead of what you do have.

Go ahead and make a list of all the things you
want. Get a piece of paper and write them all down.
Don't hold back. Make a good healthy list. How
long is it?

Now get a separate piece of paper and write
down all the things God has provided for you. Write
them all down.

Did you remember to write down your health
and the ability to see, touch, hear, taste, smell and
breathe? Remember, every breath and heartbeat is a
gift from God. Did you forget that? What about
the ability to walk, run, jump and play. Did you
write those down or did you forget? What about

the friends that God has given you? Did you include them? What about all the things God has pro-
tected you from? Did those make your list?

Share your list of God's provision with your
family. Encourage them to make a list either in writing or just popcorn out thoughts as you think of
each of the blessings of God. A thought from one
person will spark another thought from someone
else until you have a longer list together than any of
you would have alone.

It is so easy to forget all the things God has provided. That is why the first thing you must do is to
always remember that God is faithful and good.
You don't serve a God who withholds blessings. You
serve a God who freely bestows His blessings upon
you in more ways than you can even count. You are
not a man in want or need. You are a man who has
been given much. So quit walking around with a
chip on your shoulder saying, "If I only had . . ."
God has given you a ton, and now He has given you
a child! What more could you possibly want or
need? So, remember.

Choose

At the end of the day it comes down to a choice. You
have to choose whom you are going to serve. It is an
unavoidable choice. But God gives you the freedom
to choose. You will have to choose multiple times a
day. Are you going to live life God's way or not?

Choose. Are you going to serve the world or God? Choose. Are you going to show your child how to be a godly person? Choose. Are you going to teach your child to love sports more than God? Choose.

Everyone has made bad choices at some point in life, choices they wish they could make over again. The choice you make whether to live your life God's way or not is going to be the biggest choice you will ever make. You do not want to know the number of parents I have had in my office over the years saying, "I wish I could go back and do it over again." Many of them live with the costly consequences of those choices still today. I do not want that for you or for your child. That is why I'm not watering this message down or holding back.

I do not want you in some pastor's office, years from now, saying, "I wish I could go back and do it over again." You have a huge opportunity in front of you right now, and it all comes down to a choice. "Choose this day whom you will serve. As for me, and my household, we will serve the LORD" (Joshua 24:15).

On the other side of the coin, I have also had the privilege to watch hundreds of dads who have chosen to live life God's way, leading their children to accept and follow Christ themselves. I have watched these dads baptize their own children who are making a public profession of their faith in Christ, and many of these dads have looked at me in that moment and simply said, "It just doesn't get any better than this." If you think about it, what could be better than leading your child to make a decision that will determine whether he or she ends up in heaven or hell! Of all the things you can choose to teach your children, is there anything more important than this?

Let's Talk Man-to-Man

- What are some things God provides that you take for granted?
- What is something you want to teach your child(ren)?
- If you could do something over again, what would you choose to do differently?
- Have you chosen to live life God's way? If not, why not?

Commit

I love the response of God's people, "Far be it from us to forsake the LORD to serve other gods!" (Joshua 24:16). That is commitment! They were not afraid to let everyone know it. Deuteronomy 6:13 reads, "Fear the LORD your God, serve him only and take your oaths in his name." When a person makes an oath, he is making a lifelong commitment, much like the type of promises you made on your wedding day to your spouse.

In the same way, you, dad, need to make a public and lifelong commitment to being a God-following dad. Do not be ashamed to admit it. Never back down or away from your commitment. If you're a fan of a certain professional sports team, you are not ashamed to admit it, nor will you ever back down or away from that commitment.

I am a lifelong Chicago Cubs, Bears and Bulls fan. I have all the paraphernalia to prove it and I will never root for another team ahead of my beloved Bulls, Bears and Cubs. I have lived in Minnesota Vikings country, but I didn't care. I wore my Bears jersey proudly. I now live in Los Angeles Dodgers country, yet I still put on my Cubs uniform and go cheer my Cubbies whenever they come to play the Dodgers. Do I take a lot of grief and ridicule, especially when the Dodgers take the Cubs out in the playoffs, which just about killed me? Absolutely! But do I care? Not a bit. I am committed to my team.

Can you be as committed to loving and serving the one true God as you are to your favorite sports team? Can you stay committed to following God even when you get ridiculed for it? You clearly have the ability to commit yourself to something. Will you commit yourself to God?

You see, it needs to go beyond a choice. It needs to be a lifelong commitment where living our faith is something that is simply ingrained to the point that it will not change no matter what. Ridicule, scorn and temptation will not make you veer off your path. You are committed to doing life God's way no matter what.

Bless Your Children

My wife and I have a ritual of praying over and blessing our daughter every evening. The ritual began after we heard a speaker by the name of Rolf Garborg tell the story of how blessing his daughter had impacted his life. He began the ritual of blessing his daughter from the first day she came home from the hospital. Every evening he would go into his daughter's room and place his hand upon her head and say, "May the Lord bless you and keep you. May the Lord make His face shine on you and be gracious to you. May the Lord continue to look upon you with favor and give you peace. I love you. Amen."

He talked about how he did this through the years, even though he was tempted to stop at times. He continued to bless her even when she was a teenager, but he said that many times during those years he would wait until she was already asleep before he would go in and bless her.

The dreaded day finally arrived when Rolf and his wife had to take their daughter to college. They decided on a plan to make the parting less painful. They would pack up their daughter's stuff and put it in the minivan. They would then take her to the college and help her set up her dorm room. Once that was done, they would have one, and only one, tearful good-bye. Then Rolf would grab his wife's hand and they would leave without looking back. Rolf said the plan worked to perfection. They set up their daughter's dorm room and had their tearful good-bye and then he took his wife's hand and they marched down the hallway, down the stairs and were halfway across the parking lot with the mini-van in sight when they heard their daughter's voice yelling to them, "Mom, Dad, wait!" Rolf said that for a fleeting moment he thought his daughter had changed her mind about going to college! "Mom, Dad, wait! You can't go yet. You forgot to bless me." And there in that crowded campus parking lot the three of them huddled together and Rolf simply said, "Honey, may the Lord bless you and keep you. May the Lord continue to make His face shine on you and be gracious to you. May the Lord continue to look upon you with favor and give you peace as you take this next step in your journey. Amen."

After hearing that story, Maria and I decided to start blessing Malyn every night, and we have faith-fully done it ever since. Over the years we have fallen into our own ritual where my wife blesses Malyn and I pray with her each evening. And on most evenings, when my daughter goes to bed, she will yell out to both of us, "Mom, Dad. I'm going to bed now." This is her code for "Get in here to bless and pray with me!" You have no idea how many times I have been tempted to not pray with her. I could be watching a good television show or basketball game and Malyn will make the announcement, "Dad, I'm going to bed now," and I think to myself, *Not now! The game only has a few minutes left. I can't leave now."*

But I go into my daughter's room and we start talking and sharing prayer requests with one another, and the next thing I know, 20 minutes has passed, I've missed the end of the game and I don't care one bit because that was the best time of my day.

Be careful of the things that will take you away from your responsibilities as a dad focused on raising your children for Christ. Bless your children through your words and your actions every day.

Let's Talk Man-to-Man

- What are some things that you are committed to?
- What drives your commitment? Why are you committed to these things?
- How strong is your commitment to living life God's way and being a godly dad? How does your life, calendar and daily activities reflect this?

5

In the Future

*In the future, when your son asks you, "What is the mean-
ing of the stipulations, decrees and laws the LORD our
God has commanded you?" tell him: "We were slaves of
Pharaoh in Egypt, but the LORD brought us out of Egypt
with a mighty hand. Before our eyes the LORD sent mirac-
ulous signs and wonders—great and terrible—upon Egypt
and Pharaoh and his whole household. But he brought us
out from there to bring us in and give us the land that he
promised on oath to our forefathers.*

DEUTERONOMY 6:20-23

Take a little time to look into the future. Your children grow up very quickly. It seems like my daughter was three years old yesterday, and now she's a
teenager! When did that happen?

Questions from Kids

Deuteronomy 6:20-23 begins with a question from
a child, "In the future, when your son (or daughter)
asks you, 'What is the meaning of the stipulations,
decrees and laws the Lord our God has commanded

you?'" One of the primary roles you play as dad is answer man. Your kids are going to come to you with questions. Your answers will shape them and their worldview.

In the future, when your son or daughter asks you, "What does it mean to be a Christian?" what are you going to say? When they ask, "Why do we live our lives according to 'What would Jesus have us do'?" what is your answer going to be?

I'm sure if they were to ask, "Why do we cheer for the Cubs or da Bears?" they would receive a very passionate and compelling answer. Do you have the same type of passionate and compelling answer for why you are Christians, living life God's way?

How about this: "I would love to tell you why we are Christ followers and committed to doing life God's way. You see, we are all going to die, and none of us knows when. I don't want to die and I don't want you to die; but no matter what we say or do, we cannot avoid death. Death separates us and keeps us from spending time together doing the things we like to do together. Isn't that sad? Well, God thinks that is sad, too, and He doesn't want death to be the end of us having fun together; so He did something about it. God sent His own son, Jesus, to stand in our place for our sins, taking our punishment on Him all the way to death on the cross. But He defeated death and sin when He rose up from the dead on the first Easter morning. And now the way has been made for us to spend all eternity together with Jesus . . . because the sin that kept us from God was taken away. When we believe in Jesus and follow His ways, everything is right between us now and forever. In God's Word it says, 'God so loved the world that he gave his one and only Son, that whoever believes in him shall not perish but have eternal life' [John 3:16]. So I'm a Christian and I live my life God's way for two reasons: First, I want to meet Jesus face-to-face so that I can thank Him personally for defeating death for me. The second reason is so that I can spend all eternity with you in heaven."

I like the way *THE MESSAGE* states the question: "The next time your child asks you, 'What do these requirements and regulations and rules that GOD, our God, has commanded mean?' tell your child, 'We were slaves to Pharaoh in Egypt and God powerfully intervened and got us out of that country'" (Deuteronomy 6:20-21). Did you notice who is supposed to provide the answers to the God questions? You are! Too many men abdicate this responsibility to either their wives or the church. For some reason men do not engage in faith-talk with their children. The primary reason I hear from men is simply, "I don't know how."

Dads today are not bad, but they are unprepared, especially in this area. You may feel very comfortable talking to your kids about sports, cars, politics and your recent round of golf. Yet when it comes to talking about God, the Bible and questions of faith, you may either change the topic or leave the room. You might even say, "That's something you should ask your Sunday School teacher." But the problem is this: Your kids don't want to know what the Sunday School teacher thinks. They want to know what you think. The answer you give is going to be two to three times more influential than any answer they will hear at church.

The Greatest Influence

In my early years as a youth and family pastor I thought everything revolved around me and what happened at church through our church programs. I thought I was supposed to be the spiritual champion for the kids in my youth group, and my attitude was pretty much, "Give me your kids—and parents, don't even bother getting out of the car, because I know what I'm doing; plus I'm cooler than you are." Of course the parents were like, "You want my kids? Gladly! Here they are. Good luck." The programs on the outside seemed to look successful as we had fairly large number of youth attending; but then God changed my entire perspective.

One day, I received a survey questionnaire that I was to give to the youth in my program. The survey was entitled "The Most Significant Religious Influences Survey."[1] It was a national survey conducted by Search Institute[2] to help determine what the factors were that influenced a teen to be a Christian. In my mind, someone was trying to discover why *my* kids in *my* youth program had faith, so I knew this was a very important, and potentially dangerous, survey. I strategically waited to give the questionnaire to my students until after we had been on a youth trip together where I did everything with them, because this would ensure that I would score highly. I collected the surveys and sent them in as instructed.

It took months to get the results, yet I still remember receiving the envelope with the words, "Survey Results Inside." I was on my way to a youth board meeting, so I thought this would be the opportunity of a lifetime. The results would clearly show that I, their esteemed Youth and Family Pastor, would be the number-one influence in their kids' faith journey. I even thought these results would strengthen my case for a raise!

At the youth board meeting I opened the letter and began to read the results. The most significant religious influence for Christian teens today is "mom." At first I was upset, but then I quickly rationalized that no one can compete with mom, so let's just chalk that one up and move on. The second most significant religious influence for Christian teens today is "dad." (Dad is always number two, so just get used to it!)

Now this one was a huge surprise to me. I had been around most of these teenagers' dads, and I spent more time with their kids than they did! How

Chart 1 Mainline Protestant Youth Most Significant Religious Influences[1]

MOST SIGNIFICANT RELIGIOUS INFLUENCES	Percent Choosing as One of Top 5							
	GRADE						GENDER	
	7th	8th	9th	10th	11th	12th	M	F
Mother	87	75	77	72	75	75	81	74
Father	64	51	55	49	57	51	61	50
Grandparent	36	28	29	34	27	22	30	29
Another relative	11	12	14	16	12	7	13	12
Siblings	22	14	13	13	15	14	18	14
Friends	22	24	28	25	31	31	22	29
Pastor	60	56	49	45	36	49	57	44
Church camp	23	30	26	25	23	23	20	28
Movie/music star	3	3	4	4	2	2	4	3
Christian Education at my church	23	30	25	25	31	25	26	26
Church school teacher	29	27	17	23	20	23	26	21
Youth Group at my church	25	25	32	33	33	34	30	30
Youth Group Leader at my church	13	11	20	17	17	15	15	16
Youth Group outside my church	3	6	2	3	4	5	4	4
Youth Group Leader outside my church	2	1	1	3	4	4	2	3
The Bible	25	30	27	23	16	26	24	25
Other books I have read	2	3	4	4	3	4	3	4
Prayer of meditation	9	15	15	16	20	18	11	19
School teacher	3	5	2	2	3	6	3	4
Revivals or rallies	3	3	4	4	5	4	3	4
TV or radio evangelist	2	·	1	·	·	·	1	1
Worship services at church	10	10	10	16	14	15	12	13
God in my life	3	3	11	11	13	13	8	13
Work camp	·	1	4	2	5	5	3	3
Mission study tour	0	0	·	0	1	1	·	·
Retreats	7	12	16	20	17	18	11	17
Coach	2	2	3	3	4	4	4	2
Choir or music at church	11	12	8	9	11	6	7	12

* Includes mainline Protestant youth only (CC, ELCA, PCUSA, UCC, UMC) weighted by congregational and denomination size.

could their dads possibly be more influential than me, their beloved and adored Youth and Family Pastor? My heart continued to sink as "Youth group leader at my church" was way down the list. It was at that point that God humbled me and pointed me to a reality that I had not seen before: Mom and dad are two to three times more influential than any church program. When it comes to faith formation in children and teenagers, kids look to their parents. "For all their specialized training, church professionals realize that if a child is not receiving basic Christian nurture in the home, even the best teachers and curriculum will have minimal impact. Once-a-week exposure simply cannot compete with daily experience where personal formation is concerned."[3]

So, dad, do you want your child to have a lasting faith that will stick with him/her for life? Do you want your child to have a WWJHYD faith that will impact the life decisions he or she will have to make regarding drugs, alcohol, promiscuous sexual activity and so on? Would you like your child to be a 24/7 authentic follower of Christ?

If you want them to be a fully devoted follower of Christ then I have one final question for you. Would you like a 26 percent or less chance that this happens, or a more than 80 percent chance that this happens? Go back to the previous chart and you will see that if you simply drop your kids off at church and expect church and church programs to teach them about faith, this has, at best, a 26 percent chance of working. But if you do the teaching, if you tell the story, if you answer the questions, if you engage in faith-talk, this has a greater than 80 percent chance of impressing faith on your kids' hearts for life. You need to be the ones telling the story to your kids, not handing it off to the "trained professionals" at church.

Let's Talk Man-to-Man

- Who were the people that influenced you to know and follow God?
- What do you think when you hear that you are two to three times more influential in your kids' lives than any church program?
- How are you going to influence your child-(ren) to be Christ followers?

Answers from the Heart

When my daughter was three she was asking those typical three-year-old questions. Easy things like, "Why is the sky blue, Daddy? Why is water wet? And Daddy, why is grass green?" How in the world do you answer those zingers! I could try to give a worldly answer. "You see, Malyn, the sky is blue because the sun is out there, and we are here on the earth, and over the earth is the ozone, and when the sun reflects off the ozone . . ." How many of you already know my answer is wrong? What if instead I would answer by telling the story? "Malyn, I would love to tell you why the sky is blue. The sky is blue because you have a great God who created that blue sky just for you. And you want to know why water is wet? I will gladly tell you why water is wet; and that's because God made water wet because He knew you were a kid who loves to play and splash in water. So God made water wet for you. And finally, you want to know why grass is green? I'll tell you why grass is green. God made grass green because He knew when you got a new pair of blue jeans, you really wanted the area around both your knees to be green!"

I can guess that you may be feeling a little overwhelmed at your role and responsibility of building faith in your child. You may be asking, "How am I going to do this? I never had faith conversations in my home with my parents. How am I supposed to do this with my child? What am I supposed to say?" Let's look at the Deuteronomy passage again for the answer.

> Tell him: "We were slaves of Pharaoh in Egypt, but the LORD brought us out of Egypt with a mighty hand. Before our eyes the LORD sent miraculous signs and wonders—great and terrible—upon Egypt and Pharaoh and his whole household. But he brought us out from there to bring us in and give us the land that he promised on oath to our forefathers" (6:21-23).

What do you tell your child? The story God has given you. You don't have to be a theologian. You simply have to know the story of God well enough to tell the story and be the story with your child. Don't be intimidated. You can do this. It's not that difficult. The role of the church is to be a lifelong partner, not a replacement, to help you know and tell the story. Let me be perfectly clear: I am not an anti-church guy. I am not saying that church or church programs are unnecessary. I think they are critically important. Gathering with other believers builds and strengthens your faith. These meetings are meant to be a reinforcement, to help you know and share the story with your children. But the primary place through which faith is nurtured is in your home, living life moment by moment with your family as you follow God's ways.

The Role of the Church

I need the church and so do you. The church helped me tell the story to my three-year-old daughter when they taught me to begin the ritual of blessing her in our home. This ritual continues to this day and she now blesses me before I get on a plane to travel anywhere. The church helped me tell the story to my daughter when she was four by teaching us how to pray with her at mealtime, bedtime and anytime. The church helped me tell the story to my child at every stage in the journey, including helping me now talk to her about dating, kissing and sex—topics, by the way, that I was totally unprepared and uninterested in discussing with her.

But thanks to the church, we were able to talk about how to approach these things God's way. The church has been a huge resource for us. But at the same time, I'm not asking the church to do my job for me. I don't want them to do that. That's my job, my opportunity, my blessing.

The church is not a drop-off center, and we can't blame the church if our kids don't have a lasting faith. I love the quote from my friend and mentor Dr. Rollie Martinson of Luther Seminary. He shared it at a conference we were both speaking at. I think it paints a great picture for the relationship that should exist between church and parents: "What we ought to do is let the kids drop their parents off at church. Train the parents and send them back into their mission field, their homes, to grow Christians."

Let's Talk Man-to-Man

- How ready are you to lead your child to accept the salvation Jesus offers, and teach him/her to follow Christ?
- Who are you going to turn to for help in this area?
- What are some things that scare and excite you about the future?

Notes

1. Reprinted with permission from *Effective Christian Education: A National Study of Protestant Congregations.* Copyright © 1990 by Search Institute SM. Used by Permission of Search Institute. No other use is permitted without prior permission from Search Institute, 615 First Avenue NE, Minneapolis, MN 55413; www.search-institute.org.

2. Search Institute is a nonprofit, nonsectarian research and educational organization that advances the well-being and positive development of children and youth through applied research, evaluation, consultation, training and the development of publications and practical resources for educators, youth-serving professionals, parents, community leaders and policy makers. Phone: 1-800-888-7828. Website: www.search-institute.org.

3. Marjorie Thompson, *Family: The Forming Center,* rev. ed. (Nashville, TN: Upper Room Books, 1996), back cover.

A Final
Man-to-Man Time

*The Lord commanded us to obey all these decrees
and to fear the Lord our God, so that we might always
prosper and be kept alive, as is the case today. And if we are
careful to obey all this law before the Lord our God, as he
has commanded us, that will be our righteousness.*

DEUTERONOMY 6:24-25

I don't know about you, but when it comes to being a dad, I want to get it right. What will be our righteousness? What is the right way to do this? Deuteronomy 6 has given us lots of food for thought and action. Read through that chapter again and again. Determine to be a faith-at-home focused dad. Don't relegate your God-given privileges to the church or to their mom only. Be involved. Be proactive. Be the man God created you to be. Be a faith-at-home focused dad where you:

- Are personally in love with God.
- Live for God at home, at work and wherever you go.
- Remember God in the busyness of the world.
- Continually tell the story of God and His faithfulness to you.

Have a working partnership with a faith-at-home focused church that equips you to:

- Know the story.
- Tell the story.
- Be the story at home, work and play.

That, my friend, is the key to you and your children and your children's children enjoying long, everlasting life! Continue to allow God to shape you into the dad He wants you to be for the children He has blessed you with.

May the Lord bless you and keep you. May the Lord make His face shine on you and be gracious to you. May the Lord look upon you with favor and give you peace as you carefully obey all the things the Lord has commanded you.

Acknowledgments

I want to thank all the people at Gospel Light who have faithfully supported the Faith@Home movement, even before it was a movement. They committed themselves to create resources like this that help men be godly dads at home. I especially want to thank my editor, Jean Lawson, who not only edited this resource but also provided some of the great ideas as well. And finally, I want to be sure to give credit to our Lord and Savior Jesus Christ who is the one that deserves all the credit for anything that is gained through this resource. God is my inspiration. I am simply an instrument through which He has chosen to work.

MARK A. HOLMEN

To find out more about Mark Holmen's speaking
engagements and to learn more about the
Faith@Home movement, visit faithathome.com.
Mark is available to speak to parents and church
leaders about how to be a faith-at-home focused
individual, family and church. For more information,
please contact Mark at mark@faithathome.com.